Changing Seasons

Rebecca McConnell

Presentation by *BookLeaf Publishing*

Web: www.bookleafpub.com

E-mail: info@bookleafpub.com

ISBN: 978-93-95755-59-7

First edition 2022

This book is dedicated to Suzanne Pepper -
my beautiful mother.

Enough?

When will I ever be enough?
Pretty enough,
Smart enough,
Funny enough,
For someone to love.

Why was I not enough?
To love,
To hold,
To care for,
Even, for just a minute longer.

When is enough, actually enough?
Of feeling hurt,
Of feeling unwanted,
Of feeling despised,
By those that utter nothing but false truths.

I seek solace to that which;
Consumes me,
Haunts me,
Terrifies me,
When will I FINALLY be enough?

Five Deep Breaths

In. Out.
Coal-black ink stains the once snowy
pillowcase,
Bronze-coloured capsules promise finite
happiness,
Tissues litter the ground like leaves in the
Autumn,
Wrinkles carve out the spines of well-worn
books,
And a shroud of dust covers the neglected bears.

In. Out.
The velvety blanket envelopes my skin,
The fan gives birth to a steady stream of
lukewarm air,
The coarse carpet chisels indecipherable patterns
across my back,
And matted hair sticks to my damp cheeks.

In. Out.
Screeching car horns,
Lilting voices of Hollywood stars,
And the too loud whispers of my inner thoughts.

In. Out.

The floral scent of spilled perfume,
And the rising sun's dewey fragrance.

In. Out.
And the briny tang of tears that remain on my
tongue.

Sorrowful Sea

Sorrow is the sea,
Sinking deeper into pitch-black depths.
Wave after wave crashes over me,
Can only take shallow breaths.

Despair is an ocean,
Briny liquid filling my lungs.
Miles of water in all directions,
Woeful thoughts go forever unsung.

Sorrow is the sea,
Piercing cold numbs the heart.
Does anyone notice?
Starving scavengers tearing flesh apart.

The Girl in the Photograph

She stands tall,
seemingly confident
and self-assured.
A Colossus of Rhodes,
watching over
the cerulean waters,
or is she simply
averting the gaze
of disapproving stares?

Azure eyes,
glistening with unshed tears.
Laughter echoes silently
from the smile
plastered across her face.
No one spies
the violent blotches
buried beneath
strawberry blonde locks.
Despondent thoughts
roll endlessly over her
like the waves
pummelling the shoreline.

Dainty fingers

crave the warmth
of the blazing sun.
Searching desperately
for the light
she wishes
to one day
own.

Blue

Blue is the Ulysses butterfly;
soaring erratically through the sky.
Evading a beguiling fox,
seeking to entrap me in Pandora's box.

Blue are the flickering flames;
cobalt waves designed to maim.
Choosing to embrace the danger,
now virtually strangers.

Blue are the forget-me-nots;
wondering why our garden was left to rot.
Blossoms cruelly clipped by your shears,
resulting in a waterfall of tears.

Blue has transformed into the cloudless sky;
unfurling my broken wings and taking flight.
A heavenly blank slate,
finally ready to explore my glorious fate.

Human Parasite

Razor-sharp words,
hooking into fragile flesh.
Pilfering all shreds of self-worth
that I once possessed.

Growing, spreading, thriving;
tunnelling through veins.
Inner thoughts deteriorate
as you penetrate my brain.

Callous comments carve
into delicate organ tissue.
Coughing up hate like crimson blood.
How long will this continue?

Nothing but a hollow shell,
too frail to resist.
Years and years of greedily consuming
all I had to gift.

Thunderstorm

9

Her guttural screams,
Iron cloak dousing starlight,
A deluge of tears.

The Mask

Smooth, ivory skin,
perfectly concealing every sin.

Scarlet lips curled in a smile,
disguising melancholy with grace and style.

Cerulean orbs dazzle in the light;
no one ever notices her eternal fight.

Dichotomy of Light and Dark

Darkness
Cold isolation
Tirelessly searching
Pain, lies, truth, hope
Bathing all in its glow
Warm contentment
Light

Once Upon a Fairytale...

Once upon a time,
that's usually how they begin.
There was a princess, elegant and divine.
Held hostage by the vile villain;
awaiting a prince, so handsomely designed.

One fateful day that prince did come;
heroically climbing the lofty spire.
"I shall once and for all thwart that witchy
scum!"
he bellowed deeply for all to hear.
With a swish of his sword turning the villain to
crumbs.

And I bet you could guess what happened next;
The enchanting couple lived happily ever after.
Well in truth, I am utterly perplexed!
There are just too many plot lines
that make NO SENSE!

Why is the princess always so meek and mild?
Why can't she be her own heroine?
She is more than just some delicate, silly child.
And what if the prince is not the saviour but the
villain?

Deceiving us with his bewitching smile.

He play-acts as the valiant knight,
professing his undying love.
Though the princess embraces her beloved tight,
he ultimately slips through her fingers;
stranding her in a heart-rending plight.

Alas, 'happily ever after' is not awarded to us by
fate.
There is no extraordinary love, gallant prince or
lavish palace.
Instead we endure reality's heartache, hardship
and hate.
Do I hope one day I'm proven wrong, and all
those tales were true?
Of course, I secretly long for that
much-anticipated date.

The Seashore

Balmy, golden rays
dawn on the soft sand
squeaking between my toes.

Crystal blue waves
lap lazily to and fro;
white foam hugging the coastline.

The taste of salt
lingers in the breeze,
clinging to my tousled curls.

Shrill cries of hungry seagulls,
desperate for forbidden sustenance,
echo off the palm trees.

Once deafening thoughts taper off,
dulled by Mother Nature's acoustics.
At long last, my mind is ready to set sail.

The Undisturbed House

The house appeared to lay undisturbed.
No voices raised in harsh discourse;
no snorts or snores emanated from bedrooms;
no minuscule creatures scurrying across cool
floors.

The house appeared to lay undisturbed.
Yet a solitary figure sat,
enveloped in the darkness,
struggling to calm her internal war.

The house appeared to lay undisturbed.
Expect for this lone soldier,
being feasted upon by maddening whispers,
rapidly transforming into roars.

The house appeared to lay undisturbed.
Though deep, heaving breaths
could almost be detected
outside the peeling bathroom door.

The house appeared to lay undisturbed.
However, a faint sniffling
emanated from the exhausted fighter;
her blaring thoughts becoming harder to endure.

The house was suddenly disturbed.
A resounding, sorrowful cry
tore through the once silent building,
impossible for the inhabitants to ignore.

Growing Sapling

17

Sapling
Fragile, youthful
Flourishing, Transforming, Venturing
An abundance of opportunities await
Evergreen

Changing Seasons

Disrobed trees
stand exposed
in the windswept woodland.

Frigid frost
encases blades of grass
like a serrated blanket.

Biting breezes
thrash wildly,
sending creatures underground.

Fracture lines form
in the icy sky
as shafts of light pierce through.

Once shivering creatures,
sniff hopefully at the warming air;
stepping tentatively outside their doors.

Blossoms bloom underfoot,
transforming the frosty ground
into a kaleidoscopic duvet.

Towering trees
look regal
in their emerald attire.

Words

Words are razorblades,
carving deeply into
delicate flesh.
Leaving behind grisly scars
for all of those whole-hearted
to bear witness.

Words are punches,
pummelling the shit out of you
with every breath you dare take.
Leaving behind hideous bruises
that bear resemblance
to the everlasting love of a bellflower.

Words are pills,
coursing through your veins.
You're enthralled;
overcome by the intoxicating messages
electrifying your brain.
Yet within only an hour, numbness reigns.

Words are candles -
fragrant spells
luring you out of the darkness.
Yet that solitary flame
can still ensnare you,
burning you from the inside out.

Drunk

was I just an intoxicated phone call?
the girl you would ring
when you felt all alone
in the cab ride home.

was I merely an inebriated text?
the girl you would contact
when all your friends
were gone.

why didn't you call more when you were sober?
when I was deflated,
tears carving steady streams
along my cheeks,
and all I asked for
was to hear
your voice.

now...
each night,
my phone sits by my bed
awaiting your
drunken call.

Jigsaw

pieces of me
are strewn
across the tiles.

a variegated mess of
red,
grey,
blue,
green and
yellow.

pieces that don't
appear to fit together
anymore.
edges that are
jagged,
curved,
straight.
whilst others seem
fuzzy,
disappearing before my glassy eyes.

some pieces
have vanished altogether;
lost,

gone forever.

how will I piece myself
back together?
how will I be
the picture perfect girl
once again?
maybe
I was never whole
to begin with.

Item Unknown

what could it be?
that vile,
crimson,
fleshy
mass.

pulsating unsteadily,
whilst scarlet liquid
oozes out
onto the pavement.

a faint wheezing
can almost
be heard issuing
from the thing itself.
taking its last
breaths of air,
fast approaching
death.

what could it be?
why,
it's a bleeding heart,
of course

Time

people constantly
reassure me,
that time heals all wounds.
so I
scan,
gaze,
study
the long,
obsidian eyelashes
that flick sluggishly
around the clock's
mocking face.
but wounds still bleed,
dripping crimson
down my body.

my aching heart
yearns
to turn back
the hands of time.
reverse the clock,
before the scars
began to set.

others stress

that time
is on my side.
but I am a
bruised and
battered
fighter,
struggling against
the clock.

I fear I am
wasting time;
watching it
slip between my fingers
like fine sand.

time and time again,
the same lesions
reopen;
pain ripping me in half.
I continually hope
it's time for a change,
and my afflictions
will one day heal.
only
time will tell.

New Chapter

The fog grey hardcover is unyielding,
binding the colourless, fraying pages together.
Plot lines culminate in the same conclusions,
repetitive,
and mechanical.
The protagonist is lost,
forever stranded
in an undulating sea of despair.

Wait...
a new chapter emerges.
Emerald letters spring forth
from the crisp, white pages.
Our protagonist hesitantly approaches
a glistening coastline,
fearing it is only
a heavenly mirage.
But no,
a new adventure
lies waiting.
Bright beams of hope
rain down
from the once
foggy sky.